F.I.T.
FINANCE

F.I.T.
FINANCE

Helping Millennials
Save, Spend, and Splurge

SALVATORE PONZIO, MBA

Patience Media LLC

Ordering Information:

Special discounts are available on quantity purchases by corporations, associations, and others. For details, contact the publisher: info@PatienceMedia.com.

Edited by Mikel Benton
Book design by DesignForBooks.com

Printed in the United States of America

To my parents,

Sal and Judy Ponzio

Contents

Acknowledgement

W hile always interested in finance and the workings of the stock market, I realized my true passion is to help others achieve financial success. As I navigated through my career, I've had tremendous mentors help me along the way. However, it was not until I was faced with a daunting decision to make a career enhancing move, when I started to wonder, "What is the best way to make a decision?" We make decisions constantly, but I never actually studied the best way to make a decision. While attempting to use the best information available, I stumbled across a few books regarding how humans think and make decisions.

Upon reading the first couple of books, with the aim of helping to make a better decision, I started to realize how fascinated I became with the study of human behavior. Moreover, the study of behavioral finance, or the study of how people treat money and what lies behind the true motives driving financial decision making.

As I began to actively read as much as I could on this topic, it drove me to realize that I wanted to communicate these findings to all my friends and family. In my mind, the best way for me to do this was to write down my thoughts, which eventually became the book you are now reading. I hope you enjoy it!

I wanted to first thank my parents for being such great role models and for always teaching us to be fair and do the right thing. I will never be able to repay them for all they did for my siblings and me. Additionally, they taught us how to work hard, be grateful, and, of course, the golden rule: "Do onto others as you would want done to you." I could not have asked to be raised in a better way than my parents raised me, in the town they raised me in, and even down to the street they raised me on.

Looking back, I learned more than I could have ever imagined from my childhood, and it helped shape me into the person I am today (which I hope is a good thing). As would be expected, my parents supported my siblings and me in any pursuit we desired—so it was no different when I started writing this book; they continued to provide support. Without their guidance and support, I do not know where I would be. I cannot pay them back enough for all they have done.

Secondly, I want to thank my brother (Joe) and my sister (Gina) for always being there for me whenever I needed them. My siblings and I were very close growing up, which allowed me to learn so much from them. We all have different skill sets and personalities, which always made for such great times when we were all together. They always kept me on my toes with great conversations about various topics, of which they both typically knew more than me, but I always enjoyed them!

I also want to thank my mentors at Lockheed Martin and Ernst and Young. Without their guidance and support, I would not have had the motivation or courage to write this book. Lastly, I want to thank my business partners and close friends who continuously give me support. Without their guidance and support, this book would have never been written—for that I owe them all a great thanks! Friendships are extremely important and valuable to me; I get great pleasure and enjoyment from my friendships. Furthermore, my friends/business partners have always been there whenever I needed to bounce ideas off them and kept me grounded by injecting humor.

My highest hope is for you to enjoy and implement this template I've created. I hope to enhance your life through better financial decisions.

What is F.I.T.?

A fter many years in the financial world and many years in the fitness industry, I started to notice behavioral similarities that seemed to work well in both professions. These similarities both were mental and involved areas of behavior that could be changed; mainly involving willpower, incentives and discipline— all which can be learned by anyone! As I continued to experience success in both fields, I wanted to expand the application of these tips and tricks that worked for my clients. I started to think of ways that I could spread this message to a larger audience. **My purpose with writing this book is to help invigorate the world to live a better life by making better financial choices.**

I started out with the idea of writing a blog and starting a website, but that didn't seem to be enough for what I wanted to say. I wanted to contain all my thoughts into a single area. I soon realized a blog post was not the proper medium. I would not be able to retain the attention of the reader long enough to fully deliver my message. So instead, I decided to write this book.

What is F.I.T.? F.I.T. stands for Financial Interval Training.

At a high level, this concept deals with the notion of implementing small changes for short time periods. The aim is to start examining our daily routines and look for areas we can improve. The F.I.T. concepts come from a fitness concept called *interval training*—which is intense bursts of effort followed by short rests. Typically, intervals are about thirty seconds or one minute. For example, you would perform an exercise at a high intensity level for thirty seconds then rest for thirty seconds. The thirty seconds "on" and thirty seconds "off" is typically repeated a number of times consecutively.

Now how do we apply this to finance?

My goal with this book is to design a template to show you exactly how to do this. But first, we will discuss where we are now and focus on the financial situation in the United States. From there, we will discuss a bit of human behavior and examine spending habits. Then we will cover topics regarding savings rates, the F.I.T. concept, and investing. Additionally, you will notice a long-term mantra throughout this book that focuses on applying small, short-duration changes that will compound over time into large, positive impacts.

With that, in the sincerest way, I hope this book can serve as a template to help you live a better life and build long-term wealth!

What three things are you doing **Today** to build your long-term wealth?

ONE

Where are we?

*It is easier to resist at the
beginning than at the end.*

—LEONARDO DA VINCI

B y setting clear goals, focusing on what
you can control and finding the right role
models, you can achieve Financial FITness. Later
in the chapter we will touch on the details, but
first I want to examine where we are now.

After reading an article by Quentin Fottrell
(director of personal finance at MarketWatch)
that cited a Google consumer survey showed 62
percent of Americans have less than $1,000 in
their savings accounts and 21 percent do not have
savings accounts, my interest was piqued and I

asked myself, "How could this be?" I pondered how an economy with a gross domestic product of nearly $20 trillion in 2018 (gross domestic product, or GDP, is simply the total sum of all products and services produced by a country within a year) could have a significant amount of its population with less than $1,000 in their savings.

As I continued to read articles and research this topic, I discovered this problem was worse than I imagined. Not only were Americans saving less, they were accumulating debt at record amounts. This truly frightened me. In addition, I realized student loan debt amassed to $1.4 trillion. These high student loan debt levels, coupled with historically high credit card debt and zero savings, seemed like the recipe for financial disaster.

Recently, I came across a report by CBS's Jill Schlesinger, which showed that the rates of Americans over the age of sixty-five filing for bankruptcy soared to the highest levels ever experienced in the history of our country. Furthermore, seven million Americans are ninety or more days late on their car payments—this number is higher than it was during the Great Recession of 2008. After noticing a pattern that seemed to be trending in the wrong direction, I felt compelled to act. So my action lead to the decision to write this book. I understand that each situation/circumstance is unique and some people fall on hard times, I do not want to give the impression that everyone can easily save money—but my goal is to *help people improve their current financial situations.*

Before we go any further, I just want to cover a few important topics I discuss when meeting with a new client or helping a friend:

F.I.T. PRINCIPLE 1

Set clear and detailed goals.

▶ Personally and financially—what do you want to achieve over the next one, five, ten years? Take fifteen to twenty minutes and truly think about what you want out of life, then jot down those ideas on a sheet of paper. These are rough, high-level ideas. When you are eighty years old, what story do you want to tell? Will you have regrets?

▶ Seriously, what do you want? Fear aside, if you could do anything—what would that be?

▶ How will you get there? What will you do each day and month to make progress toward your goal? What most people do not often realize is that small wins will amount to huge victories. Set small tasks and goals and watch your success take off. For example, if your high-level goal was "I want to become a dancer," then a more defined goal could be "I will attend five auditions and I will connect with ten people in the industry by December 1st."

▶ Small goals include simple daily action items. For example, read for ten minutes or exercise three days a week. The important part is to build off it and do not get discouraged if you miss one day. We all make mistakes!

▶ What are you good at? What do others compliment you on? What are you bad at? What should you avoid?

F.I.T. PRINCIPLE **2**

FOCUS INTENSELY ON
WHAT YOU CAN CONTROL.

▶ People place too much emphasis and energy on things they cannot control. Instead, we

should be dedicating our energy and effort
to things we can control.

▶ If you cannot directly impact a situation
or an outcome, pay less attention to that
situation.

▶ Everyone must play the cards they are
dealt—how will you play your hand?

F.I.T. PRINCIPLE 3

EVERYONE NEEDS ROLE MODELS.

▶ Who are your role models and why?

▶ What five words would you want someone
to use to describe you?

▶ What five words would you want people to
avoid when describing you?

▶ Ensure that your habits reflect how you
want to be described.

What you do and how you act every day is
what you will become. Examine your current
actions and behaviors. Do these habits align with
your long-term goals or the person you want to

be? Keep in mind the quote by Leonardo da Vinci and start forming good habits and behaviors now because it will only become harder the longer you wait. There is no easier time to change than now.

Keep in Mind

▶ Change is easier the earlier you try to change.

▶ Role models are important; they serve as "voices of reason" and help keep you on track.

▶ You choose the habits you form.

TWO

Why do we spend?

Compound interest is the eighth wonder of the world. [Those] who understand it, earn it . . . [Those] who don't . . . pay it.

—ALBERT EINSTEIN

P rior to examining ways to curb our spending habits, I feel it is important to understand what primarily drives our spending patterns. What we do with our money and how we spend it is the single most important driver to long-term wealth. Obviously, earning money is essential to build wealth. However, saving is the difficult part; it is the discipline to resist spending and resist the social urge to spend that takes self-control and a focused effort. Spending money without regard and not tracking where your money is going is the easy part, everyone can do that. This aligns with a mantra I hope you see throughout this book, which is to avoid the herd mentality, stay focused on the long-term, and be an independent thinker.

With that being said, the good news is that controlling and tracking your spending takes less than one hour per month and mostly everyone can do it.

Throughout this book we will show you how to do this. You can do this. You will do this. I know it! So before we go any further, I want to present the following scenarios. After carefully reading each one, please choose the scenario you think will generate the most wealth.

SCENARIO 1

Sam understands the importance of saving and investing money and decides to start saving after graduating high school (at the age of nineteen). Sam takes the time to think about a realistic dollar amount that can be saved each year. After writing out a more detailed plan and setting up a budget, he realizes that the number he originally thought of is too high. Sam reconsiders his first number and elects to save $1,800 per year. He then decides to invest, earning an annual return of 10 percent.

After saving his money for eight years, compounding at a 10 percent rate of return, at the age of twenty-seven and decided to stop investing any future money into his account. Sam decided to work in a field that did not require a college degree and has zero student loan debt. He no longer contributed another dollar into the investment account.

However, Sam allowed the money to ride in the investment account which continued to compound at 10 percent each year, until he retired at age sixty-five.

SCENARIO 2

Pat understands the importance of saving and investing money. She values education and decided to work hard to earn good grades with the hope of getting accepted into a highly desirable college after graduating high school. As it happened, she was accepted to the school of her dreams. Pat started saving money for books and living expenses as life for college was fast approaching. Upon graduating, she accepted a well-paying position at a well-known ad agency.

While understanding the importance of saving, Pat was faced with student loans and living expenses. She decided to put off retirement saving until further along her career path. Fast-forward a bit, Pat successfully climbed the corporate ladder and, at twenty-seven years of age and decided to start investing $1,800 annually in a retirement account earning a 10-percent return each year. She planned to save more in the future, but for the moment was focused on paying down student loans and enjoying life.

Unfortunately, Pat never got around to increasing the annual contribution in the retirement account, but did continue to invest the original $1,800 per year from age twenty-seven until retirement at age sixty-five (earning a 10-percent compounding return on the invested money).

Now that you have read both scenarios (and perhaps done some calculations), which scenario would result in more wealth over the long term? Pat who saved for *thirty-eight years* or Sam who saved for *eight years*? And the answer is: Scenario one will end up with more wealth. Sam will end up with more wealth even by only saving for eight years versus Pat's saving for thirty-eight years! The compounding growth effects are extremely impactful to long-term wealth, as alluded to by the Albert Einstein quote at the beginning of the chapter.

To take full advantage of this incredible phenomenon, you will need to save early and often. Therefore, I would argue that the ability to spend less, which frees up your cash to save more, will have an enormously positive impact on your well-being and long-term wealth. There is no better time to start applying and leveraging this amazing concept than now. If you have not started yet, do not fret about it, just start today and be grateful that you started. We will further discuss throughout this book ways you can get started.

As we saw in the previous example, saving an enormous amount each year is not required (if you save early) to accumulate a large sum of money over the course of your life. I have provided a high-level summary of the two situations below:

	Retiring at 65	Retiring at 65
	Sam	Pat
Annual Savings Amount	$1,800	$1,800
Current Age	27	27
Age Started Saving	19	27
Years until Retirement	38	38
Total Years Saved	8	38
Rate	10%	10%
Savings after Eight years	$20,584	$0.00
Total Saved at Retirement	$769,953	$655,278

F.I.T. PRINCIPLE 4

WE ALL WANT TO BE LIKED!

Our propensity to spend can be traced back to our prehistoric ancestors and survival tactics. During the early days of human evolution, the primary goal was to stay alive, and a favorable strategy in achieving this was to fit in socially. Fitting in socially caused others to like you, thus decreasing the chances others would attack you. Our primates forebearers would typically copy the styles of others to blend in and gain approval from peers.

There are two reasons this increased the likelihood of survival. The first reason resonates with the liking principal, a term coined from the psychology field, which means that people will act more favorably toward people they like. Thus, acting like someone else increases the chances of being liked, which in turn decreases the chances of being attacked or killed by a rival group (increasing survival). The second reason deals with strictly survival: primates who were living obviously were successful at avoiding death. So copying their strategies seemed logical to avoid their own deaths (similar advice would be, "Don't take money advice from those who are broke").

As we have evolved as human beings, we have advanced beyond the point of worrying about survival in our day-to-day lives. However, these evolutionary behaviors are deeply rooted in our human makeup and still exist today. This helps explain some common ideas, such as the herd mentality (people will do things solely based on the fact that other people are doing it), conformity, and conflict avoidance (humans feel an extreme comfort with going along with others and an extreme discomfort from disagreements or conflicts with other humans).

In the United States and other developed counties, most citizens have the fortunate pleasure of access to clean water, shelter, and food. However, the desire to be liked and fit in socially remains. If you are someone who thinks they do not care what others think of them, then I would ask if you would be willing to publicly display (for others to see) how much you spend and save each month. I would encourage you to act as if you must publicly display your finances, how much debt you have, how much you are saving, and how much you spend. If you started behaving as if you had to publicly display your finances, I think this would change some behavior!

I make this claim about being liked based on spending patterns among Americans. If humans acted as rational agents and did not try to be liked or fit in, they would have no other justification in purchasing exorbitantly priced tennis shoes, clothes, and other non-essential items that go in and out of style at the cost of taking on expensive debt. In addition, buying overpriced coffee, over-spending at bars, or trying to impress a person you find attractive via spending all support my claim that people want to be liked and fit in and will spend foolishly to achieve approval. I very much understand celebrating and rewarding by spend-ing money for enjoyment—my comments here pertain to folks who are in extreme debt and con-tinue to spend lavishly.

For example, you could spend $200 on a pair of tennis shoes and less than two years later (even though the shoes are still in great condi-tion) spend another $200 on a pair of shoes, just because your favorite celebrity or athlete wore them, and they were "cool."

If you think about, you can buy a pair of shoes that cost $40 and will do the same job as the $200 pair of shoes, with only a slight difference in quality. (Think about if you invested the $160 differential into a fund and watched it swell—talk about opportunity cost.) But we want to be liked, we want others to think we are cool, so we will follow the crowd and overspend for simple items.

This example goes well beyond what I just mentioned; think about designer watches, clothes, handbags, etc. As we will see throughout the course of this book, human beings operate on emotion. Human beings are complex emotional creatures who do not always operate rationally. I realize some people are in more fortunate financial situations and can afford higher-priced luxury items. In some cases, there is a clear quality premium for the higher-priced item. However, in most cases there is not a huge difference in quality relative to the price paid. For the record, I tip my hat to all those who have been successful and have earned enough wealth to make these purchases and enjoy the fruits of their hard work—I applaud your efforts and skill!

Overall, I understand that we are all human beings with complex psychological makeups and emotions and that we are living in a very complex world. My aim here is to shed light on what drives irrational spending and how humans behave. I still want you to have fun and enjoy life, but take a more balanced approach.

Some examples of this include the following:

▶ Instead of getting a five-dollar latte six times a week, aim for two or three times a week.

▶ Purchase a gym membership for only the winter months, you can you can exercise outside the other times of the year.

▶ In lieu of going out to bars or restaurants every weekend, go once or twice a month. Your friends will still be there even if you do not attend every night out (and if they are not, then they were not your friends in the first place) and it will become more enjoyable.

I propose living a life of balance with a more disciplined approach to spending. This should increase the propensity to save, thus increasing your long-term wealth.

The good news is that what I am suggesting is not impossible to follow, and I will provide helpful tips along the way. What I am suggesting is a change in behavior that most people can achieve. I am not asking you to be six feet eight, bench press four hundred pounds, or cycle in the Tour de France. I am simply suggesting implementing small behavioral changes that only require small amounts of effort and attention. These actions should yield an enormously positive impact on your entire life.

F.I.T. PRINCIPLE 5

Jealousy and Envy

As we continue to examine what drives spending habits, I want to shift the focus to jealousy and envy. This aligns with our F.I.T. Principle 4 because due to the fact people want to be liked, they get jealous of others who might be more likeable or have material items they want. Said differently, humans tend to want what they cannot have and having something others cannot possess creates feelings of jealously or envy.

This type of thinking aligns with keeping up with the Kardashians or trying to keep up with your neighbors or peers by trying to impress them with the material things you purchase. However, I would argue that we should shift the focus internally and be grateful for what we have and stop worrying about keeping up with a specific image. Life is too short, and that style of thinking is too hard. Less is more. Keep it simple and you will enjoy life much more.

Although it is healthy to strive for improvement and seek achievement, which could involve using others as motivation, we should not let

jealously be the engine that drives irrational
spending behavior. Acting this way could be
associated with being materialistic or getting a
large portion of your self-worth from purchasing
items. A better use of our time would be to ask
those people you are jealous of how they got to be
successful and learn from them. Most successful
people are more than willing to help others.

In my opinion, social media has exacer-
bated jealousy and envy. This has caused others
to become more judgmental and allowed more
opportunities to be jealous. To further this point,
I would argue that social media has driven us
to become less productive. Spending more time
on social media leads to accomplishing less and
increases emotions like jealously and envy. Consider replacing time spent on social media with
time spent on starting a business or learning a
new skill.

Social media drives this phenomenon
because the less you accomplish, the lower your
self-esteem. This increases the chances that you
will feel jealous emotions. As we spend the majority our free time occupied by screens instead of
being productive, our propensity to be jealous
increases.

Furthermore, in Philip Kotler's book *Marketing 4.0*, he states that during waking hours

Americans check their phones nearly fifty times per day or nearly every twenty minutes. Constantly checking your phone can lead to a feeling of loneliness, because instead of interacting and having authentic and deep connections you are having shallow and superficial connections. This perpetuates jealously of others and depressed feelings about yourself.

When feeling jealous and depressed, you will be more inclined to spend irrationally to make yourself feel better. Even if you think this does not happen to you, your subconscious is constantly absorbing and remembering everything you view and take in. So when you are scrolling through your social media feed and thinking "Wow, they are living a great life—I want to be like that," those emotions and thoughts are being recorded by your subconscious.

These thoughts and emotions continue to be reinforced as you are consistently scroll through social media. This eventually becomes a self-reinforcing pattern that will cause you to feel less about yourself, resulting in the increased inclination to spend irrationally because you are feeling jealous and depressed. Again, if you do not believe this happens to you, there are many studies that show the negative impact on your brain of high phone use, more specifically social media.

The preferred behavior would be to do things that strengthen your brain (reading, mediation, solving complex problems, being kind, etc.). I do see some benefits of social media (marketing, networking, etc.), but these highly addictive apps need to be viewed in moderation. One must consider the pros and cons when evaluating their screen time. I would recommend and encourage more live interactions with one another.

Lastly, please remember people are only posting their best life on social media. People can control what they post and choose to only post the very best parts of their lives. The majority of people will not post failures or mistakes.

As Americans, we live decently, relative to other countries. In general, Americans have clean drinking water, shelters, and access to food. When it comes to spending behavior, I would argue that we need to focus on ourselves and limit the constant comparison to others. This will allow us to live within our means and avoid being one of the Americans with less than $1,000 saved.

A great start is to ask why and how things are priced so excessively and examine the trade-off between short-term purchases and long-term wealth. This is an area where we need to apply long-term thinking. For every dollar we spend, we must earn that much more money to cover the increase in spending. So if you buy something for $200, you must consider where are you going to earn an additional $200. This is something to consider, especially when purchasing high-priced items. If you buy a television for $3,000, how can you earn an additional $3,000 (assuming you do not have the cash saved)?

As we saw earlier with the Sam and Pat example, incremental savings can lead to enormous amounts of wealth. We will examine this further in the investment section. For now, I want to bring this to your attention since the opportunity cost is high when you spend your money. Think about how much a $3,000 purchase could cost you in twenty years.[*] I personally wish I would have learned this concept earlier in life!

F.I.T. PRINCIPLE 6

PLANNER VS DOER

At this point in our evolutionary journey, the knowledge of how to stay healthy and in shape is

---

[*] $3,000 invested and earning 10 percent for twenty years is $20,150.

commonly available to most. However, we face an obesity epidemic in the United States. How can this be?

As health awareness continues to increase, with a focus on being active and eating healthy, people are still becoming obese and unhealthy. If knowledge is increasing and more people are aware, then people must change their behavior. The decline in health in general is not due to a lack of information, therefore, we must avoid falling into patterns of behavior that decrease health. Furthermore, I am quite sure most people do not set goals to be overweight and unhealthy. This tends to happen over time as we create unhealthy habits or show lapses in willpower.

Conversely, some folks set goals to lose weight, but sometimes the goal is not achieved. We will explore why this is in a moment, but first I wanted to point out that this same phenomenon can be applied to savings. I am quite sure most people do not set goals that include spending all their money and having less than $1,000 in their savings accounts!

Yet in the largest economy in the world, roughly half of the population cannot withstand a $400 surprise expense—this is according to Tim Ryan (congressman, Ohio) in a recent interview. So if the required information for staying healthy is widely known and it is common knowledge that saving money is a good thing, why are Americans not fit with relatively low amounts of money saved? I will lean on thoughts from a Nobel Prize-winning behavioral economist (and one of my favorite authors), Richard Thaler, for some help to explain.

Thaler and Cass Sunstein do a brilliant job explaining the complexities behind human behavior in their book *Nudge*. In the book, the authors present how the brain has two separate operating systems, also called planner or doer. I will keep this brief since 1.) *Nudge* does a much better job of explaining this concept and 2.) this book is not intended to go deeply into human psychology. However, if you happen to have read *Nudge* and enjoyed it, *Thinking, Fast and Slow,* by Daniel Kahneman is the best book I ever read on human behavior and judgement. I highly recommend it.

Back to our systems 1 and 2. System 1 can be thought of as our subconscious, our intuition or gut feeling. System 1 is constantly processing information and generating thoughts by combining past experiences with current situations. System 2 is the logical operation that processes thought and attempts to control System 1. If I asked you to multiply 54 by 19, your system 2 would be activated and exert effort to do the mental calculation. System 2 arguably is a filter for system 1, which is constantly bouncing thoughts and ideas off your system 2. It's up to your system 2 to act as the gatekeeper.

Since I am not a Nobel Prize-winning economist, I will let Mr. Kahneman better explain systems 1 and 2. The following is a direct quote from his book *Thinking, Fast and Slow*:

> System 1 operates automatically and quickly, with little or no effort and no sense of voluntary control. System 2 allocates attention to the effortful mental activities that demand it, including complex computations. The operations of System 2 are often associated with the subjective experience of agency, choice, and concentration.

As pointed out above, these separate operating systems can be broken down into a far-sighted Planner and a near-sighted Doer. You can think of this dynamic when you are resisting temptation to do something that you know may harm you, but you continue to proceed because you gain pleasure (e.g., eating unhealthily, consuming too much alcohol, impulse spending, etc.). While you know the action will most likely not benefit you in the long run, you still proceed. What happens is that your Doer takes over and you will proceed with the negative action anyway. This is what most people refer to as *willpower*, or lack thereof in this example.

Studies have shown that willpower behaves like a muscle; it can become fatigued, injured, or stronger. The more often you exercise willpower, the stronger it becomes. However, until you strengthen your willpower, in the short term you will exhaust it. This may lead to moments of bad choices or simply lapses in willpower. I wanted to point this out, because as you continue to better yourself, there will be weak moments and setbacks. Please understand that this is simply your willpower becoming exhausted.

Eventually you will strengthen it enough to overcome these weak moments. An example would be waking up before work to exercise. At first, you exert willpower to wake up early and get the motivation to exercise. This finite willpower will become exhausted very quickly in the beginning, perhaps, resulting in a lapse a lapse of willpower later in the day when tempted with a sugary cookie or dessert ("I worked out today, so I can have this"). However, as previously mentioned, as you continue to exert the willpower to wake up early and exercise, it becomes easier and ultimately forms into a habit.

The example I just described can directly apply to mindless spending and controlling financial behaviors. Align your short-term, mindless purchase with giving in to your Doer. Instead, you should shift your thinking to align with your Planners "I told myself I would not spend money this weekend, I need to stick to this plan. I can spend next weekend." This would help you give more consideration to the purchase or behavior intended; in turn, delaying gratification or simply not giving in to the urges at all. Just by giving thirty seconds of thought to a purchase or action will have a tremendous positive impact on your life. Ask yourself, "Why am I buying this?"

When wrestling with which system or part of the mind to listen to, just remember that one must win. What I mean is this is a zero-sum dilemma where you cannot "sort of" let your Planner win. Either your Planner wins or your Doer wins. I will describe these two once more, so you can decide which you would prefer to win. Per Richard Thaler and Cass Sunstein in *Nudge*: "The 'Planner' is trying to promote wellness, happiness, sound decision making, long-term thinking and self-control. The 'Doer' is action-oriented, short-term thinking, strong-willed and constantly exposed to external temptations of pleasure."

Many of the world's troubles could be solved by understanding this simple concept and taking the few minutes to think about if our actions are aligned with our Planners or Doers. The good news is that anyone can do this. You just need to commit thirty seconds of thought before making a choice. Let your willpower and brain do the rest.

Keep in Mind

▶ Herd mentality = failure. If following the majority made you successful, wouldn't everyone be successful?

▶ Live beneath your means; build a margin of safety. Stop comparing yourself to others and keep the focus on things you can control.

▶ There is a natural ebb and flow to all things. Learn from the bad times and persistently look for the good in the downside. All things pass, and even the worst of times come to an end. We all struggle with the internal pushing and pulling of our Planners and Doers.

THREE

Budgeting and Saving

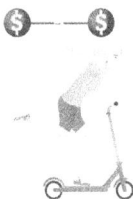

I would rather be in the business of lending at twenty percent vs being in the business of having to pay or borrow at twenty percent.

—Warren Buffet

Now that we have learned what drives spending and potential ways to reduce it, let's explore how to properly save. The most important component when saving money is developing a mechanism to track your spending: What am I spending on? Where am I spending? Firms and corporations dedicate entire departments to answering these questions. This is driven by the importance of tracking and planning your spending.

The amount of resources deployed by firms in order to maintain complete visibility and control over their spending and savings (cash inflow and cash outflow) is impressive. I know, I know, personal finance does not require an army of people with trend analyses, forecasting, etc.

The good news is that you are correct! Personal budgeting is easy and should be a bit of fun, since it's your money. However, the simplicity and ease of creating a budget strengthens the argument for it. I will share an example of a budget I use in the appendix; it is a template within Microsoft Excel. The folks at Microsoft made this process even easier by making budget templates for their users. I highly encourage you to check out the template I use or browse within Microsoft Excel for a budget template that works for you.

Before we cover the F.I.T. Principle from this chapter, I want to focus on the quote from Warren Buffet (who is one of the greatest and most successful money managers of all time). Warren Buffet is describing the credit card business. This business lends you money at approximately 20 percent to 30 percent interest rates and charges high fees for late payments. The interest is only charged on outstanding balances, but the rate is still very high.

Additionally, by using a credit card you are opening yourself up to excessive spending behavior that could lead into a vicious cycle of revolving debt. Even if you can afford the things you are buying with a credit card, there have been various studies around credit card premium that show, when all things are equal, people will spend more when using credit cards versus using cash.

Not only will they spend more, people place a higher value on items when purchasing with a credit cards. Said differently, people are willing to pay more for products when purchasing with credit cards versus using cash. Swiping a card is psychologically less painful than handing over cash. Part of the reason for this is driven by an ownership bias. People do not like giving up things or having things taken from them. When you pay with cash, you are parting ways with the dollars you spend (someone is taking something from you). Conversely, when you swipe with a credit card, the card is returned and your brain likes the way that feels better than parting with cash.

The credit card business is so unattractive for the customer, they have to offer very favorable incentives to lure customers into signing up. Some of these perks include small discounts on purchases, money back, airline miles, etc. I would ask you to add up all the "perks" you receive from credit card spending. Then compare those perks to the increase in total spending due to buying on credit. In most cases you would be far better off without the perks and spending less. But the credit card companies know how to lure you into thinking, "This is a great deal. I am getting 5 percent cash back on gas." Meanwhile your over-all spending had increased by an amount that exceeds your income.

If you spend $2,500 on gas per year, you will receive around $10 per month in "cash back" benefits. Is that worth the risk of overspending?

The revolving credit cycle usually starts out small, with amounts you can pay. Then, over time, the amounts may start to increase and when they do you will start paying 20 percent to 30 percent on your outstanding debt. Now the compounding interest effect is working against you, not for you as we saw in the example in the beginning of the book with Sam and Pat. Their money was work-ing for them to grow each year. When you rack up credit card debt, it also grows by 20 percent to 30 percent each year. Moreover, the growth rate that Sam and Pat experienced was 10 percent, the rate of growth for credit card debt is two or three times higher. We saw how big of an impact a 10 percent percent growth rate can have over time. Think about the negative impact of a 20 percent to 30 percent growth rate to debt.

These extraordinary high percentages became such a large problem that the government had to step in. Credit card companies are now required to disclose the financial details of debt; they did not do this by choice. *Part of the disclosure requirement included the amount of time a balance would be paid off by only making the minimum payments.* However, even with a good amount of data supporting why credit cards are not beneficial to your financial wellbeing, people make the argument that credit cards are much more convenient that cash.

That is exactly what the credit card companies want. They want to make it *easier* for you because the more you spend, the more money they earn. Some people argue, "I only use my credit card for fuel and groceries" (or whichever items offer the most cash back). By doing this your willpower is tested and, as we previously saw, maintaining willpower and self-discipline is not particularly easy. I would argue to forgo the perks in exchange for eliminating the temptation to spend more by having the credit card. You will be better off financially and save more money. In addition, with the rise of payment apps and debit cards, I would argue that credit cards should become less popular.

Lastly, what value does your credit card bring? Think for a moment about the positives of your credit card. Try to name five positives of owning a credit card. If you are like most people, you probably struggled to name five positives to owning a credit card. Perhaps online shopping was one of the positives that came to mind. I share the same thought that credit cards make it easier to shop online (although with the rise of other payment methods, credit cards are becoming less critical to online shopping), but how can you use a credit card for only online shopping and resist overspending?

To help provide a solution to this, I will rely on my business partner. His approach was uploading his credit card information to the desired website, then cutting up his credit card. This allowed him to no longer physically possess the card, but still allowed him to make online purchases that he needed (of course, you must make sure your credit card does not have an annual fee). I thought this was a great way to keep the upside convenience of online shopping, while removing the downside temptation to spend excessively with a credit card.

F.I.T. PRINCIPLE 7

WHAT IS YOUR SAVINGS RATE?

People in the financial world tend to focus on rate of return, or how much money you are earning on the money you have invested. I tend to focus on *savings rate*, with the mantra of paying yourself first. I like to think of saving money as the rate you pay yourself, instead of saving. When depositing cash into your bank account, you are actually "paying yourself" instead of spending it.

In his video *The Economic Machine*, Ray Dalio refers to this as one person's spending being another person's income. Every time you spend your cash, you are increasing the income of another person, while decreasing your wealth. The reason for this is simply because when you spend money you are transferring your wealth from yourself to the entity you purchased from.

I have broken out savings rate into two definitions because I think each definition is equally important. First, we will examine *retirement savings rate*. This is simply the amount saved into your Roth 401k, traditional 401k, or other retirement account (this will be covered in more detail throughout, but I encourage you to work with a financial professional when making this decision). Furthermore, I would encourage you to focus on a savings percentage of income vs an absolute dollar amount. For example, instead of saying, "I'll save $50 a pay check or pay period," I would suggest shifting your focus to, "I'll save 10 percent per pay paycheck or pay period."

The reason I prefer percentage amount over absolute amount is because percentage is much easier to plan for; it's much easier to add a couple of percentage points to savings rather than trying to pick another absolute dollar amount. So if you save 8 percent of your pay to a Roth 401k and 8 percent to a traditional 401k, your total retirement savings rate is equal to 16 percent.

The second savings rate I define is *personal savings rate*, the total amount saved divided by net income. For example, let's assume that your net pay (after taxes, healthcare, etc.) is $1,000 per month and you save $100 per month, then your savings rate would equal 10 percent ($100/$1,000). As previously pointed out in the example of Sam and Pat, focusing on savings rate is the most important thing you can do for your financial wellbeing.

I want to share some good questions to ask yourself each year regarding savings rate:

▶ What is your savings rate?

▶ Do you have one?

▶ Do you know it?

▶ Have you developed a savings rate goal?

▶ Do you have a plan to achieve this goal?

If you did not answer yes to these questions, that is absolutely fine because the good news is that very little time and effort is required to change the no to a yes. Just by asking yourself this question and developing goals driven by a budget (as we will see in the next F.I.T. Principle), you will be far better off than you were before.

F.I.T. PRINCIPLE 8

SET SAVING AND SPENDING GOALS

In the previous F.I.T. Principle, we mentioned savings rate, but that is one component of your overall financial goals. Developing a savings rate and sticking to it is the foundation for all financial goals. Therefore, I decided to carve it out as a separate F.I.T. Principle. On your path to building long-term wealth you must realize and expect the journey to be slow and long—set the proper expectation.

The reason I mention this is because people I have helped in the past would say, "Saving $25 a week isn't worth it; that is too little of an amount to make a difference." However, as we have shown with compounding interest and the time value of money, no amount is too small. Keep that in mind when you develop your budget and financial goals. Do not get discouraged if you are not satisfied with your amount. Instead, I would encourage you to use a low savings amount as motivation to look for areas to spend less and earn more.

How do you go about creating a savings goal? First you need to set something that is realistic and that you can easily stick to. I recommend setting up a monthly budget, as we previously discussed, that has net cash inflow (income) and net cash outflow (expenses) broken into categories. This exercise should take no more than thirty to sixty minutes. I will provide you an easy-to-use template (all you need is access to Microsoft Excel). Using this template will put you in an excellent spot to develop an achievable monthly savings goal. Once you have done your homework by inputting all your individual information into the Excel template, you will have more visibility into how much you can afford to pay yourself.

What if you did your homework and you realize that there isn't much money left over to save?

In the expense section, you can apply more rigor to your inputs and explore areas to trim $10 here or $5 there in your spending. The elimination in spending can be as simple as reducing your daily $5 coffee down from five days per week to two or three days per week, which would yield additional savings of $10 to $15 per week. Or you can cut back any discretionary activity; however, I am not saying to eliminate all fun activities out of your life, just cut back. Instead of going out to dinner every week, reduce your frequency to twice a month.

A different savings approach altogether is something I refer to as *Financial Interval Training*, one of the most important concepts in this book. Let's define financial interval savings, which involves eliminating something from your life in short increments, typically one to two months. The concept of financial interval savings comes from my personal training background. It's relatively common for trainers to apply interval training to workouts designed for their clients, which are simply intense efforts followed by complete rest.

An example of interval training for fitness would be thirty seconds of intense activity immediately followed by a rest period of thirty seconds. This type of effort yields superior results to other styles of training. From this, I started to think about how I could apply this type of mindset to other areas in my life and stumbled into financial interval training.

An example of financial interval training (intense periods of savings, followed by normalized spending) would be to eliminate certain spending habits for non-essential items in short durations. Examples include eliminating online purchases for one month, giving your credit card to a family member or trusted friend for one month to eliminate excessive spending, not buying coffee every day for a week, or not going out to dinner for two weeks.

This will result in elimination of the undesired behavior or activity for a short period of time, with the emphasis on short durations to increase the chances of removing the selected behavior or activity because the goal is easily achievable. Once that month, week, or day passes, you can revert to living your normal life. I would encourage you to focus on one area at a time and then continuously rotate which areas you choose to focus on. For example, perhaps you will not dine out for an entire month; once that month passes you can resume your normal schedule of dining out. Then replace dining out with eliminating buying clothes or accessories for an entire month, and once that month passes you can resume your normal habit of buying.

As you can see, we are only making short efforts of change, but if you continue to extrapolate this forward each month, you will notice substantial results to your wealth over the course of one year.

The method previously described can be applied in any part of financial planning and is not limited to one-month intervals. I would suggest starting small, with two-week increments then working your way up to months and then years (maybe). I started applying this theory to my financial life and experienced wonderful results. I would urge you to think about the costliest discretionary items in your budget and apply the financial interval savings approach to those items.

To further underscore this point, let's say that you buy various items throughout the month. I would suggest stopping all purchases for one month, or maybe two weeks. Then track the results in your budget spreadsheet. You will be delighted with the results. This will allow you to explore different ways to save and create small wins, which in turn will have profound positive impacts on your life.

F.I.T. PRINCIPLE 9

WHAT HAVE YOU ACTUALLY
SAVED AND SPENT?

Track your performance. This is a principle we take from management which states that if you cannot measure it, then you cannot improve it. This concept is very popular in management textbooks and for good reason. All professions must be able to clearly and accurately track their results; this is the basic way to understand whether what you are doing is working. Otherwise, you will have very little insight into what drives improvement and what to avoid. I realize we have touched on this subject throughout the book thus far, but due to the importance of tracking your performance, I want to address this subject in a separate F.I.T. Principle.

In sports, coaches, fans, and players obsess over statistics and the tracking of those statistics. In baseball, fans place a significant amount of weight on batting average when determining a player's ability. A low batting average equates to a poor performer, while a high batting average equates to a high performer. The same argument can be made across all major sports: when evaluating a player's ability, the first area people examine is tracked performance.

Tracked performance is also heavily used in the business world, health profession, and just about anything else you can think of. With major developments in machine learning, artificial intelligence, and more access to data than ever before, the world is trending to a data-driven society.

I want to highlight that tracking performance has never been easier in our history and we should use that to our advantage. As previously mentioned, I've added step-by-step instructions on how to access a template to track your spending and saving performance. I would encourage you to take thirty minutes and populate the template with your information. From there, just simply update each month, spending no more than twenty to thirty minutes updating once you start tracking your spending each month. I would spend no more than twenty to thirty minutes updating each month. You will inevitably discover areas where you can reduce spending. This is the magic of tracking performance.

Keep in Mind

▶ Avoid debt and excessive spending on credit cards. This creates the financial equivalent of quicksand.

▶ Savings rate > rate of return; define and continuously revisit your target savings rate. Apply the financial interval savings method to inject a boost into your financial well-being!

▶ Take thirty to sixty minutes every year and review your financial health. What did you spend on? How much did you save? What was your savings goal? How can you increase it?

FOUR

Investing

The desire to get rich fast is pretty dangerous, my own system was to get rich slow and protect my wealth.

—CHARLIE MUNGER

Now that we have covered ways to curb spending and ideas around budgeting and saving, the last step in building long-term wealth is investing. I want to cover this topic last because it is vital to develop good spending habits and focus on establishing a budget that is easy to stick to prior to investing. Additionally, once you have done the upfront work, investing can be as easy or as difficult as you would like. I would encourage just about everyone to make it as easy as possible. We will dive into what this means in much more detail throughout the chapter.

Before we go any further, if you do not recognize the name Charlie Munger from the quote, allow me to introduce him. He is a business partner of Warren Buffet and his net worth is approximately $2 billion. More than that, Munger is very intelligent and possesses a tremendous amount of knowledge and wisdom. He is a philanthropist, a leader, and a wonderful man.

F.I.T. PRINCIPLE **10**

Passive investing
(Stocks and Bonds)

To start, I wanted to define a stock and a bond:

Stock: An ownership stake in a company (*not* pieces of paper that get traded back and forth), typically signified by shares, giving the shareholder(s) rights to profits of the business.

Bond: A loan to a company, carrying a rate of return that coincides with the risk of repayment by the debtor.

Passive investing is the most advised way to invest in equities for a couple reasons—it takes virtually no effort and yields satisfactory returns. What I mean by no effort is that you can set up a portion of your income to go into a fund that someone else manages for you or a fund that holds or tracks a basket of equities. There are a variety of these funds, but it's advisable to pick the fund with the lowest net fees, which are clearly reported by the fund. For example, you can buy the Standard & Poor's 500 exchange-traded funds, which is a fund that tracks the performance of and invests in the top 500 stocks in the stock market without any effort on your part. This is a great way to earn good returns without ever thinking about which stock to pick.

It's worth mentioning that some employers offer certain funds to their employees, although often the number of funds offered is overwhelming and can become confusing. I want to strongly advise working with someone to help sift through the funds, or picking the S&P 500 option is a reasonably good choice. Additionally, to mitigate risk, you do not want all your money in one single fund. Try to pick three to five different funds to ensure that you are properly diversified. **The main points I want to emphasize is: do not let the feeling of being overwhelmed discourage**

**you from putting your money into a retirement
account and do not put if off until later**.

The longer you wait, the more difficult it
becomes to change your behavior. This decreases
the likelihood of your starting to invest each day
that you delay your choice to invest. Furthermore,
after becoming aware of the profound impact of
time and starting early (as we saw at the beginning of this book), why wait? Take action now!

Again, I want to emphasize that this takes
no effort on your end after the initial set up and
if you work for a company that provides a 401k
plan, then they will assist—just ask. What if you
do not work for an employer that offers retirement vehicles? Not to worry, because you can set
up individual retirement accounts through any
large financial institution that offers these types
of services. They are very easy to find, just do a
quick search on the internet. The only hurdle
here is taking the initiative to set it up. If you
just call the desired institution, they will walk
you through it and help pick sound investments
for you. Or you can work with a financial advisor
to help get you started. The emphasis here is just
get started.

I want to provide a quick snapshot of some
popular retirement vehicles with the aim of helping you to become more familiar, which in turn

will increase the likelihood of your making a better choice.

▶ *Traditional 401k*: An employer-sponsored retirement plan that reduces your taxable income by the amount of money invested. For example, if you make $50,000, the government will tax you on the $50,000. However, if you contribute $10,000 to a traditional 401k account, then your taxable income reported to the government is $40,000 ($50,000 salary minus the invested amount of $10,000). This is a wonderful tax advantage provided by the government to incentivize retirement savings. The downside is that you will pay taxes on the amount you withdraw from the fund when you reach retirement age. I won't get into too many specifics here, but the point is that you can defer tax payments until you start withdrawing from the account. (Please consult with a financial professional for a much more detailed explanation as this goes beyond the intended scope of this book.)

▶ *Roth 401k*: An employer-offered retirement plan that is funded by after-tax money. For example, any amount you contribute to your Roth 401k is money you have already paid taxes on. Think of this as your net pay on your pay stub; it's like taking your net pay and then directing a specified amount to the Roth 401k account. At first glance, this seems inferior to the traditional 401k because of the lack of tax benefits. However, with a Roth 401k your money grows tax free and you do not pay taxes when you take a distribution.

For a more direct comparison, let's assume that you have amassed $500,000 in a Roth 401k and $550,000 in a tradition 401k. The $500,000 in the Roth 401k is all yours and you will not have to pay any tax, but the $550,000 in the traditional 401k is taxable—let's say at 20 percent. So now each time you take money out of your traditional 401k you must pay 20 percent to cover your tax liability. In total you can assume that the $550,000 is now worth $440,000 or 80 percent of $550,000. This reduction is partially offset by the tax savings you were able to enjoy by reducing your taxable income while investing into your traditional 401k.

▶ *Individual Retirement Account (IRA):* A non-employer-sponsored plan that works very much like the aforementioned 401k accounts. You will just need to set up these on your own through the proper financial institution.

Since these different vehicles offer different benefits, I think it's wise to contribute to both. This will allow you to take advantage of short-term tax reductions while enjoying long-term tax-free distributions when you retire; in other words getting the best of both worlds. Arguments can be made to support different views on the two different 401k vehicles, but as the premise of this book is to keep everything simple, I am also keeping my analysis of this simple.

The general guidance is to aim to save 15 percent of your income for retirement, broken up as you desire (one possible split would be 7 percent in Roth 401k and 8 percent in a traditional 401k). Another benchmark for retirement is to have two times your salary saved by age thirty-five. Don't, don't fret if you currently do not have that amount saved—like I said, "benchmark." You still have time to adjust your savings rate to achieve the desired benchmark.

As I mentioned earlier, by passively investing in equities and keeping pace with the overall
market, you will do extremely well. This is what
I was referring to as "satisfactory gains." You do
not need to have spectacular gains in order to
amass a good amount of wealth. You simply need
to do average over a long period of time, with the
emphasis on starting early, and implementing the
F.I.T. model to increase investment contributions
. . . then just wait! Let the power of compounding
growth take over.

Some people struggle with this. They struggle
to do nothing once their money is invested, even
though doing nothing and letting their money
sit in the funds they have selected yields greater
returns over the long term.

Most people feel compelled to act. One of
the most difficult things in the investment world
can be holding equities as the stock market plum-
mets. I want to reassure you that selling when
stocks are plummeting is not advisable. The main
reason for this is because it's too difficult to time
the market. Folks have a hard time determining
their re-entry points into the market once money
is pulled out. Therefore, I strongly encourage you
to stick to your plan and continue buying as you
normally would (think back to our Planner vs
Doer analogy). Staying on track and continuing

to purchase as planned is one of the best things you can do as a long-term investor, as we saw in the two scenarios in the beginning of the book. There is not a thirty-year period since the inception of the stock market in which returns were negative or people lost money over that time frame.

With that being said, let's refer to the example I used at the beginning of the book, with Sam and Pat letting their money earn 10 percent each year. By simply keeping up with the stock market you will earn approximately 8 percent each year. (The historical return of the S&P 500 is approximately 8 percent.) So not panicking over short-term gyrations of the stock market and letting your money sit will yield great results!

S&P 500

Source: Macrotrends, "S&P 500 Index—90 Year Historical Chart," https://www.macrotrends.net/2324/sp-500-historical-chart-data.
*Note that if you kept your money invested through the 2008–2009 crisis, you would have made your money back in a few short years. Be a long-term investor; don't irrationally pull your money out!

F.I.T. PRINCIPLE 11

ACTIVE INVESTING (DON'T DO IT)

A different approach to investment is trying to actively select individual stocks and bonds on your own merit. I want to say this now: this is extremely difficult, and I would heavily advise against this approach. Highly educated people all around the world spend countless hours with the best resources and connections trying to beat the market through active investing. Most of these people fail or do not consistently outperform the market over numerous years; very few do, but the majority fail.

I want you to put this into perspective when considering which investment approach to take. There are much better things to do than dedicating the time and energy to attempting to outperform the stock market. The much easier route is passive investing. I want to emphasize this even more by drawing attention to the difficulty with active investing. There are thousands upon thousands of brilliant folks who spend an enormous amount of time trying to beat the market. Most of these folks fail. I am most likely not doing active investment justice by this brief overview, but avoiding active investing is the only point I am trying to make. Let the pros invest for you while you spend more time enjoying your life!

F.I.T. PRINCIPLE 12

LONG-TERM MINDSET

When thinking of an approach to almost anything in life, a long-term mindset seems to be a favorable option. Have the end goal in mind first. If you want to retire with one million dollars, then what are the steps required today for you to amass one million dollars for retirement? If you want to live a long healthy life and avoid going to hospitals, then what steps are required daily for you to maintain good health? Additionally, I would encourage everyone to apply second-level thinking to all decisions.

Before we get into second level thinking, I want to emphasize long-term thinking by asking you to be long-term greedy.

What does it mean to be long-term greedy? What I mean by being long-term greedy is avoiding the gimmicks and impulses to spend money irrationally or give into short-term pressures that might seem good now, but do not make sense for your long-term wellness. Do things now that will tremendously impact you in the long term, but please recognize and accept this will not instantly satisfy you. However, you should gain great satisfaction and gratification from knowing that you are being long-term greedy.

Back to second-level thinking: Second-level thinking is looking at the second consequence as an outcome of an initial action, rather than simply the immediate, near-term first consequence. An example of this is when you think about having $5,000,000 at retirement, you know that you will need to start saving money today and continue to save over a period of time. However, if you save $100 the first month, that does not have an immediate impact. People who think short-term may give up on this strategy because they do not see immediate gains, failing to realize that if they continue to save, they will ultimately reach their goals.

Sticking to the plan and continuing to chip away at a goal takes willpower. This does not require a specific set of skills—just a shift in thinking. Conversely, second-level thinkers will realize that to achieve their goals they must stick to their thought-out plans while keeping the end in mind each month, and saving their $100. Second-level thinkers view each $100 saved as one step closer to achieving their goals and they thrive from this! So when you start thinking about decision making, start by examining the second-order consequence of the initial action you are taking. This approach will hopefully help you live a better life.

As previously mentioned, irrational spending is the core of first-level thinking. Furthermore, credit card spending is a first-level thinking view. If a person buys a high-priced item with a credit card, without the immediate funds to pay it off, they could be ignoring significant long-term financial implications (think about interest paid, debt repayment for years, etc.). Impulsivity and instantaneous satisfaction from making a large purchase make it easy for people to fall into this mindset of irrationally spending and ignoring the long-term financial impacts.

It appears that some Americans tie self-worth to how much they spend and acquiring nonessential items. This type of thinking is counterintuitive because the more you spend the less cash you possess, which could lead to taking on expensive debt. I would strongly urge you to ask yourself if you have the cash to cover the purchase. If the answer is no, then you are taking on expensive debt to cover the transaction (short-term thinking). In the end, if you cannot fully pay off all credit card debt each month, then you are spending more than you are making, without any room to save. This type of behavior is dangerous and can lead down a financially frightening path.

If you continue this type of behavior for thirty years, where will you end up? This question is linked to long-term thinking. If you continue to succumb to the short-term urges and impulses of feeding your self-worth via buying, then you will most likely end up hurting yourself in the long term.

I would encourage you to run a quick calculation that focuses on how much money you save each month and extrapolate that into the future thirty years. This can be difficult, so please seek out help if needed. After you have a rough idea of exploring where you will end up in thirty years, are you satisfied? If not, refer to some of the topics previously covered and try implementing them into your life.

I hope that some of the ideas covered in this book will help you on your life journey. I also hope that this book helps you view some topics from a different perspective and encourages you to live life better!

Keep in Mind

▶ Save early and often; the earlier and more often the better.

▶ Doing average in investing can create an enormous amount of wealth. Have patience and always keep a long-term mindset (**be long-term greedy**)!

▶ Do not actively invest (unless you are a professional money manager).

What one or two things will you start doing today to improve your long-term wealth?

CHAPTER

FIVE

The Importance
of Enjoying Life

W̲e have discussed at length ways to improve your life through better financial decisions and simple behavioral changes. However, I do not want to leave you feeling stressed and anxious, because while we are incorporating positive changes into our lives, we need to enjoy it! Life is too short not to enjoy it— enjoy the process, enjoy bettering yourself, enjoy being better off financially—which will, in turn, improve your quality of life. Furthermore, there will be times when you get off track or deviate from your plan. These deviations are totally natural, as progress does not happen perfectly.

Do not create undue pressure for yourself that will create undue stress, which can cause you to underperform. Enjoy life to the fullest (within reason). Spend time with loved ones and close friends, be kind and nice to everyone you meet, be positive and grateful. You have already taken a significant step in improving your life if you are reading this, so please feel accomplished and energized. Continue to make small improvements each day and expect setbacks. Do not let setbacks completely derail you from your goals.

The process I discuss throughout this book is not impossible and is not meant to make your life difficult, but rather to serve as a template to enjoy life and, along the way, build long-term wealth.

The aim of this book is to address the question of why half of Americans have less than $1,000 in savings. It is very alarming to me that the largest economy in the world had such poor personal financial conditions. I hope that some of the ideas contained in this short and simple guide help place some clarity on the original question. Additionally, I want to reiterate the notion of *financial interval savings* and emphasize how helpful this has been to my financial well-being.

The idea is very popular in the fitness industry and has yielded great results, which I can personally attest to. Since the results were very positive, I thought about applying this to other areas in my life, and money was the first area that came to mind. Please consider areas where you can incorporate this strategy into your own life. The best part of this strategy is the short durations. The short durations limit the inconvenience or shock to your routine and will be over before you know it. So give it a try; there is no risk. Look for a couple months or weeks each year where you can start to apply financial interval savings!

I will ask you one favor. The moment you are finished reading this book, please take one action from the book, even if you sit and think for ten minutes about where you are spending your money. Just simply take one action from this book and implement it into your life right now. This is a costless and riskless activity that could have a very profound impact on your life. There is no downside risk.

The longer you wait, the harder it is to change. You have no easier time to change than now; it will only get harder the longer you wait. "If you want to change the way of being, you must change the way of doing." I want to end with this quote because I think that anyone can change at any point in time. The only way to change outcomes or your position in life is to change your actions and behaviors. Always remember that you choose your habits, you can choose to be late or prompt, hardworking or lazy, flaky or reliable—choose wisely!

Summary

F.I.T. Principle 1: Set Clear and Detailed Goals

F.I.T. Principle 2: Focus Intensely on What You Can Control

F.I.T. Principle 3: Everyone Needs Role Models

F.I.T. Principle 4: We All Want to Be Liked!

F.I.T. Principle 5: Jealousy and Envy

F.I.T. Principle 6: Planner vs Doer

F.I.T. Principle 7: What Is Your Savings Rate?

F.I.T. Principle 8: Set Saving and Spending Goals

F.I.T. Principle 9: What Have You Actually Saved and Spent?

F.I.T. Principle 10: Passive Investing (Stocks and Bonds)

F.I.T. Principle 11: Active Investing (Don't Do It)

F.I.T. Principle 12: Long-Term Mindset

Concluding
Points to Keep in Mind

- ▶ Change is easier the earlier you try to change.

- ▶ Role models are important and serve as "voices of reason" to help keep you on track.

- ▶ Avoid debt.

- ▶ Herd mentality = failure. If following the majority made you successful, wouldn't everyone be successful?

- ▶ Live beneath your means and build a margin of safety. Stop comparing yourself to others and keep the focus on things you can control.

- ▶ There is a natural ebb and flow to all things. Learn from the bad times and persistently look for the good in the downside. All things pass and even the worst of times come to an end. We all struggle with the internal pushing and pulling of our Planners and Doers.

▶ Avoid debt and excessive spending on credit cards, as this creates the financial equivalent of quicksand.

▶ Savings rate > rate of return; define and continuously revisit your target savings rate. Apply the financial interval savings method to inject a boost into your financial well-being!

▶ Take thirty to sixty minutes every year and review your financial health. What did you spend on? How much did you save? What was your savings goal. How can you increase it?

▶ Save early and often, the earlier and more often the better.

▶ Doing average in investing can create an enormous amount of wealth. Have patience and always keep a long-term mindset (be long-term greedy)!

▶ Do not actively invest (unless you a professional money manager).

A

Time Value of Money Table

	Retiring at 65	Retiring at 65
	Sam	Pat
Annual Savings Amount	$1,800	$1,800
Current Age	27	27
Age Started Saving	19	27
Years until Retirement	38	38
Total Years Saved	8	38
Rate	10%	10%
Savings after Eight years	$20,584	$0.00
Total Saved at Retirement	$769,953	$655,278

B

Excel Budget

STEP 1 : Open Microsoft Excel and click the "New" tab.

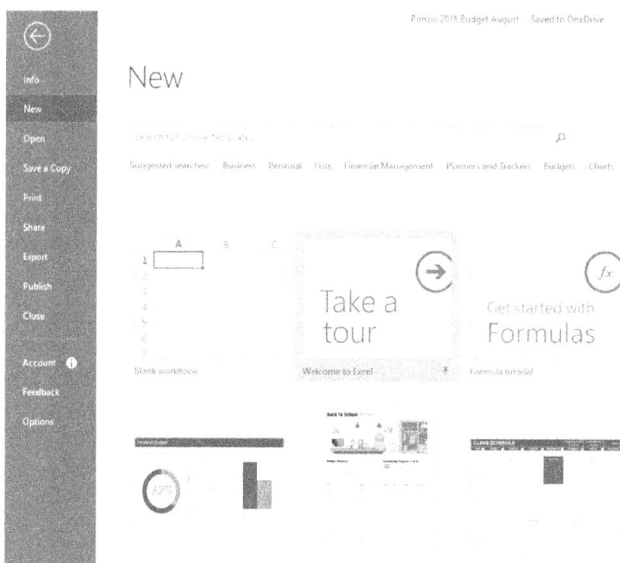

STEP 2: Click within the "Search for online
templates," type "budget," and scroll
down to the fifth row of charts.

STEP 3: Click the "Personal budget" chart
in the bottom right hand corner—
this is the budget I prefer. However,
feel free to explore other fantastic
options that might work better for
you (family budgets, co-budgets
with a roommate, etc.).

STEP 4: Populate the tabs with your
individual information.

About the Author

Salvatore Ponzio earned his undergraduate degree at Youngstown State University and his master of business in business administration from Kent State University. He started his career as a financial analyst at Lockheed Martin and currently works at Ernst and Young. Sal is also a certified personal trainer and enjoys an active lifestyle. In his spare time, Sal enjoys sports, especially golf, investing, and spending time with close friends and loved ones.

www.ingramcontent.com/pod-product-compliance
Lightning Source LLC
Chambersburg PA
CBHW031905200326
41597CB00012B/539